DISCARD

HIP-HOP & R&B

Culture, Music & Storytelling

Beyoncé

HIP-HOP & R&B

Culture, Music & Storytelling

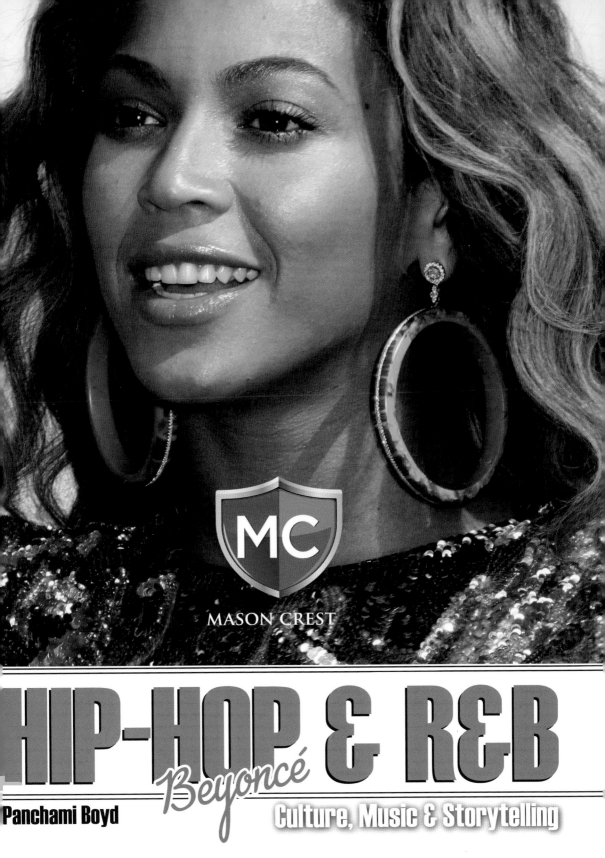

MC

MASON CREST

HIP-HOP & R&B
Beyoncé

Panchami Boyd

Culture, Music & Storytelling

Mason Crest
450 Parkway Drive, Suite D
Broomall, Pennsylvania 19008
(866) MCP-BOOK (toll free)

First printing
9 8 7 6 5 4 3 2 1

ISBN (hardback) 978-1-4222-4177-6
ISBN (series) 978-1-4222-4176-9
ISBN (ebook)978-1-4222-7619-8

Library of Congress Cataloging-in-Publication Data

Names: Boyd, Panchami, author.
Title: Beyoncé / Panchami Boyd.
Description: Broomall, PA : Mason Crest, 2018. | Series: Hip-hop & R&B:
culture, music & storytelling.
Identifiers: LCCN 2018020765 (print) | LCCN 2018022426 (ebook) | ISBN
9781422276198 (eBook) | ISBN 9781422241776 (hardback) | ISBN
9781422241769 (series)
Subjects: LCSH: Beyoncé, 1981---Juvenile literature. | Singers--United
States--Biography--Juvenile literature.
Classification: LCC ML3930.K66 (ebook) | LCC ML3930.K66 B69 2018 (print) |
DDC 782.42164092 [B] --dc23
LC record available at https://lccn.loc.gov/2018020765

Developed and Produced by National Highlights, Inc.
Editor: Susan Uttendorfsky
Interior and cover design: Annalisa Gumbrecht, Studio Gumbrecht
Production: Michelle Luke

QR CODES AND LINKS TO THIRD-PARTY CONTENT

CONTENTS

KEY ICONS TO LOOK FOR:

Words to understand: These words with their easy-to-understand definitions will increase the reader's understanding of the text while building vocabulary skills.

Sidebars: This boxed material within the main text allows readers to build knowledge, gain insights, explore possibilities, and broaden their perspectives by weaving together additional information to provide realistic and holistic perspectives.

Educational videos: Readers can view videos by scanning our QR codes, providing them with additional educational content to supplement the text. Examples include news coverage, moments in history, speeches, iconic sports moments, and much more!

Text-dependent questions: These questions send the reader back to the text for more careful attention to the evidence presented there.

Research projects: Readers are pointed toward areas of further inquiry connected to each chapter. Suggestions are provided for projects that encourage deeper research and analysis.

Series of glossary of key terms: This back-of-the-book glossary contains terminology used throughout this series. Words found here increase the reader's ability to read and comprehend higher-level books and articles in this field.

Beyoncé
HIP-HOP & R&B

Chapter 1

Beyoncé Career Highlights— Becoming a Global Sensation

All of Beyoncé's solo albums have charted at number one in the United States, selling over 26 million albums in the United States and almost 60 million albums globally. Moreover, she was a member of the group Destiny's Child, which has sold nearly 18.6 million albums in the United States and approximately 40 million albums globally. Her incredible achievements in the music industry are not only inspirational, they're also well-deserved when considering the amount of effort and dedication she puts into her art.

Beyoncé's career is filled with noteworthy moments, from starting her solo career to releasing studio albums, and participating in exciting collaborations with other artists. This chapter dives in to highlight these moments and her work as a musical artist.

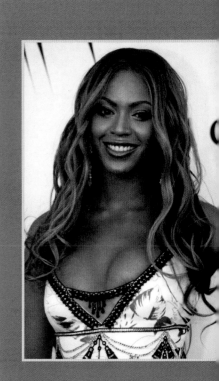

All Released Solo Albums To Date:
Discography

DANGEROUSLY IN LOVE
(Released June 24, 2003)

Beyoncé's first ever solo album was a critical success and set up her solo career in the best

Scan to watch *Crazy in Love* from Beyoncé's first album. The song was remixed and rerecorded in 2014 to be featured in the film *Fifty Shades of Grey*

way possible. The album, with fifteen songs total, debuted at number one on the *Billboard Top 200 Chart*. It has sold over 5 million copies in the United States and over 11 million copies worldwide since its release, spotlighting this great start to her individual career.

Collaborations

- *Crazy in Love,* featuring Jay-Z
- *Baby Boy,* featuring Sean Paul
- *Hip Hop Star,* featuring Big Boi and Sleepy Brown
- *Signs,* featuring Missy Elliott
- *That's How You Like It,* featuring Jay-Z
- *The Closer I Get to You,* featuring Luther Vandross

B'DAY
(Released September 04, 2006)

This album was released on Beyoncé's birthday, making the thought behind the title very clear. During its first week, it sold over half a million copies, and the album eventually went on to win a Grammy for Best Contemporary R&B Album. Since the album's 2006 release, it has sold over 12 million copies worldwide.

Collaborations

- *Deja Vu,* featuring Jay-Z
- *Upgrade U,* featuring Jay-Z
- *Beautiful Liar,* featuring Shakira

Scan here to watch *Deja Vu,* the first single released from this album

I Am... Sasha Fierce
(Released November 18, 2008)

Her third studio album performed well on the charts all around the world. She received seven Grammy nominations for the album and won six, which was the most number of wins by a female artist at the time. It sold 482,000 copies its the first week of sales, eventually topping the *Billboard 200 Chart*. It has sold over 16 million copies worldwide. Lead singles from the album, *If I Were a Boy and Single Ladies (Put a Ring on It)*, were extremely well-received. In fact, *Single Ladies (Put a Ring on It)* is the most-often streamed video on Beyoncé's YouTube channel.

Collaborations

- *Video Phone*, featuring Lady Gaga

4
(Released June 24, 2011)

Beyoncé's fourth album, aptly titled 4, was her attempt to get R&B back on the radio. She had this to say about her motivation and hopes for writing the album: "Everything sounds the same on the radio. With 4, I tried to mix R&B from the '70s and the '90s with rock 'n' roll and a lot of horns to create something new and exciting. I wanted musical changes, bridges, vibrata, live instrumentation, and classic songwriting."

Scan here to watch the music video for Beyoncé's hit song *Single Ladies (Put a Ring on It)*

The album itself was deeply personal and original, with themes to empower women and girls. The album has sold over 1.5 million copies in the United States. It was a critical success at the time of its release, evidenced by the fact it reached number one status in eight countries worldwide.

Collaborations

- *Party,* featuring André 3000

BEYONCÉ
(Released December 13, 2012)

This self-titled album was released as surprise visual album, and marked the beginning of Beyoncé taking a very strong stance in creative control over her work. She included several special pieces containing empowering messages for girls and women and other intimate subject material. Each song was released as a short film with political and personal themes, such as self-reflection. The entire project was developed in complete secrecy—all of the videos and the musical recordings. It became the fastest-selling album on iTunes when released. Since that time, it has sold over 8 million copies globally.

This was a project that highlighted the depth of excitement fans have for Beyoncé's work and cemented her ability to use unconventional tactics when releasing and promoting her work.

Scan to watch Beyoncé explain the themes in the album, her mindset and artistic vision, and behind-the-scenes moments from her self-titled visual album (Part 1 and Part 2)

Collaborations

- *Drunk in Love*, featuring Jay-Z
- *Mine*, featuring Drake
- *Superpower*, featuring Frank Ocean
- *Blue*, featuring Blue Ivy
- *Flawless Remix*, featuring Nicki Minaj
- *Drunk in Love Remix*, featuring Jay-Z and Kanye West
- *Blow Remix*, featuring Pharrell Williams

LEMONADE
(Released April 23, 2016)

LEMONADE became the highest-selling album of 2016, and all twelve tracks from this critically acclaimed work debuted on *Billboard*'s Top 100 Chart. It has sold over 1.5 million copies, and over 2 million album-equivalent copies. The visual album was released on HBO and has been lauded for its cinematic appeal, sceneries used, and the artistic vision that Beyoncé applied in its creation. Ahead of the film release, there was no prior announcement of what the video would show, adopting a similar marketing strategy to the "no promotion" release of Beyoncé's self-titled visual album. Immediately after the film played on HBO, the visual album was available to be streamed on Tidal, and was available for purchase the next day on Amazon and iTunes.

With a number of genres used in the album, Beyoncé showed off her versatility as a singer and revealed that she was willing to take risks. It

Scan here to watch *Hold Up*, a lead single from LEMONADE

demonstrated her ability to always find new ways to surprise and excite her fans, and that she was excited at the opportunity to change up her style.

One of these ways was by using spoken poetry. Beyoncé adapted Warsan Shire's poems for use in the visual album, an element that added perspective and nuance to the project's artistic appeal. The album has been praised as being Beyoncé's boldest work, taking several risks and using a number of musical styles, including country and rock. Along with winning two Grammy Awards, one for Best Urban Contemporary Album, the album also topped *Rolling Stone's* list of 50 Best Albums of 2016.

Collaborations

- *Don't Hurt Yourself,* featuring Jack White
- *6 Inch,* featuring The Weeknd
- *Forward,* featuring James Black
- *Freedom,* featuring Kendrick Lamar
- *Daddy Lessons,* on stage with the Dixie Chicks at the Country Music Awards

Other Albums

Along with all of her chart-topping studio album releases, Beyoncé also has released a number of extended versions and live versions.

She has a total of six studio releases, six live albums, three compilation projects, and two karaoke albums. This highlights that even after releasing studio-ready songs, Beyoncé looks for new and exciting ways to share her music with fans.

Live albums provide fans who didn't get a chance to attend tours the opportunity to enjoy her vocals firsthand, and gives those who attended her shows the chance to relive their experiences. It also demonstrates to fans that she doesn't shy away from the spotlight in person and will always be excited to share her raw talent.

Tours Completed

She has participated in five headlining tours, following the releases of her albums, and two co-headlining tours. The first co-headlining tour she participated in was with Missy Elliott and Alicia Keys in 2004.

Alongside their collaboration singles, Beyoncé co-headlined the On The Run tour with her husband, Jay-Z. It made over $100 million total during nineteen North American tour stops.

Beyoncé Cosmetology Center

She has also conducted three residency shows, one in Las Vegas, after which she released a DVD of the concert event. Another was held in New York City in 2011, following the release of her album 4. The final residency show was held in New Jersey in May 2012. Beyoncé has additionally performed live at a number of awards shows, including the Grammys and the Country Music Awards. She embraces opportunities to perform in person and puts together exciting and vibrant shows for her fans and viewers to enjoy.

DANGEROUSLY IN LOVE Tour

The DANGEROUSLY IN LOVE Tour was Beyoncé's debut tour as a solo artist. It had a total of ten shows in Europe. Even though some critics were displeased by her vocal range during the trip, she worked relentlessly to promote her new work.

The Beyoncé Experience Tour

This world tour, in support of her second album, B-Day, ran from April 10 to November 12, 2007. It had a total of ninety-six shows across North America, Europe, Asia, Australia, and Africa. The tour's gross profits were $90 million, and overall, it was well-received by critics.

I Am... Sasha Fierce Tour

This year-long global tour had stops in North America, Europe, Asia, Africa, and Australia, resulting in over 100 shows. It grossed $119.5 million and featured tracks from her I Am... Sasha Fierce album, as well as past solo hits and songs from Destiny's Child.

The Mrs. Carter World Tour

The year-long circuit, from April 15, 2013, to March 27, 2014, featured songs from the self-titled album following its release. Overall, the tour grossed approximately $212 million, with 126 shows during that time period. There were nearly 2 million attendees, and there were concert events in North America, South America, Europe, and Oceania.

The Formation World Tour

A month prior to Lemonade's release, its lead single, *Formation*, was released, along with an announcement about The Formation World Tour. With a total of forty-nine shows across North America and Europe, this tour sold over 2.2 million tickets. It ran from April 27, 2016, to October 07, 2016.

Teamwork Makes the Dream Work: More Noteworthy Collaborations

Outside of her own albums, Beyoncé doesn't release collaborations often, but when she does, they're surefire hits. Because they are infrequent, the buzz around these collaborations increases and the moments are more noteworthy. A few of her most popular features are highlighted here.

Put It in a Love Song by Alicia Keys, featuring Beyoncé
(Released January 19, 2010)

Alicia Keys remembers the studio experience as fun and "outrageous." Though they shot and filmed a video, it didn't quite result in the energy and mood that both artists hoped for, so they kept it on hold. In a 2016 interview, Alicia Keys teased fans by mentioning the possibility of releasing an exclusive video on Tidal. The song was certified Gold in Australia.

Scan the code to watch the full halftime show from 2016 with Coldplay, Beyoncé, and Bruno Mars

Telephone by Lady Gaga, featuring Beyoncé
(Released January 26, 2010)

This track is often considered the standout song from Lady Gaga's album THE FAME MONSTER. Nominated for a Grammy Award, it sold 7.4 million digital copies in 2010, making it one of Lady Gaga's best-selling singles.

Feeling Myself by Nicki Minaj, featuring Beyoncé
(Released December 15, 2014)

Off Nicki Minaj's album THE PINK PRINT, this single debuted on *Billboard's* Top 100 and is certified Gold. The duo also released a music video for the song exclusively to subscribers of Tidal, an added bonus for Beyoncé, a co-owner of the website.

Hymn for the Weekend by Coldplay, featuring Beyoncé
(Released January 29, 2016)

This was the second single off Coldplay's album A HEAD FULL OF DREAMS. The video and song are critically acclaimed, and it was beautifully shot in Mumbai, India. The duo also performed together at the Super Bowl XLVII Halftime Show, along with singer Bruno Mars.

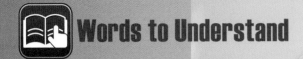
Words to Understand

chart: the charts, ratings of the popularity of popular music albums, usually based on nationwide sales for a given week.

Grammy Awards: one of a group of statuettes awarded annually by the National Academy of Recording Arts and Sciences for outstanding achievement in various categories in the recording industry.

magnet school: a public school with special programs and instruction not available elsewhere in a school district; these programs are specially designed to draw students from throughout the district.

performing arts: skills that require public performance, as acting, singing, or dancing.

single: a music recording having two or more tracks that is shorter than a full-length album; also: a song that is particularly popular independent of other songs on the same album or by the same artist.

Chapter 2

The Road to the Top—Fulfilling a Lifelong Dream

Family Life

Beyoncé was born in Houston, Texas, on September 04, 1981. Her parents, Matthew Knowles and Tina Knowles, have nothing but respect for her achievements and her hard work. She calls her mother her biggest hero, and says her mom has taught her about "caring for others, working hard and working smart." Beyoncé's father managed her band, Destiny's Child, though eventually they parted ways professionally. Her older sister, Solange Knowles, is also a singer. Solange's latest creation, A Seat at the Table, is her first number one album on *Billboard*.

Beyoncé is married to Jay-Z, a well-known and award-winning musical artist. They have collaborated on several musical endeavors, sharing in their successes and supporting each other

Jay-Z

both on a personal and a professional level. They have three children together: Blue Ivy, Sir Carter, and Rumi.

Her family is supportive, loving, and musically inclined. No matter the ups and downs they face in their personal lives, she knows she has them to count on.

High School Dropout Rates—Each year in the United States, 1.2 million students drop out of high school. As a result, several music artists and celebrities are taking a stand on the importance of staying in school and getting an education. Chance the Rapper is one such celebrity, and much of his focus has been on his hometown Chicago. He donated $1 million to Chicago public schools to fulfill students'"right to learn." He also announced the creation of a "New Chance Arts and Literacy fund" accepting donations for Chicago public schools. Contributions to the fund will focus on bringing arts programs and necessary resources to underfunded Chicago schools, giving students brand-new opportunities to succeed.

Education Matters, and Beyoncé Agrees

Beyoncé went to St. Mary's Elementary School, where she first started to take dance classes. This cultivated her interest in the arts, and she eventually practiced her talents at Parker Elementary School. This music **magnet school** was where she sang with the school's choir, and further developed her passion for singing. She also attended high schools in Houston, Texas—School for the Performing and Visual Arts and Alief Elsik High School. These educational

Booker T. Washington High School for the **Performaing Arts**

centers helped focus Beyoncé's direction in and enthusiasm for the arts, which helped set her up for success, even if that success wasn't immediate.

By the time Beyoncé was fourteen years old, Destiny's Child had signed on with Silent Partners Production, Inc. The members of the band, Beyoncé included, moved to Atlanta, Georgia, where the production company was based.

It's important to note here that Beyoncé didn't forgo her academics as her

Scan here to watch ***Flawless**, which features clips of a young Beyoncé participating in the competition *Star Search*

musical career started to take off. Instead, all four band members participated in tutoring sessions. While there, the girls balanced their academic studies along with working on their music and spending time in the recording studio.

Growing Up and First Musical Steps

Beyoncé's love for performing and singing led her to participate in local talent shows and music competitions as a child. Some of her music videos, like ***Flawless,** even include recordings of these competitions.

At age eight, she was part of a group called Girls Tyme, managed by her father. Through competitions, and as time passed, Girls Tyme morphed into Destiny's Child—eventually going on to have thirty **chart singles** on *Billboard's* Top 100, and becoming one of the most influential girl groups in history. In fact, many current girl bands—including Little Mix and Fifth Harmony—cite Destiny's Child as an inspiration for their work. Destiny's Child released its first album in 1998 and its last album in 2004. The group was nominated for nine **Grammy Awards**, and won two during those years.

Becoming a Solo Artist

Beyoncé's first solo appearance on a song was with Jay-Z on his album THE BLUEPRINT: THE GIFT AND THE CURSE. The song, *03 Bonnie & Clyde*, released in 2002. It was nominated for a BET Award for Best Collaboration and received a tremendous amount of positive support, setting Beyoncé's solo career up for success.

Shortly after, on June 24, 2003, Beyoncé's first solo album was released. DANGEROUSLY IN LOVE received critical acclaim and sold over 5 million copies in the United States in 2015. Four of the singles ended up on *Billboard*'s Top 100 Chart. Two of them reached the number one spot, and two others landed at number five.

Becoming Beyoncé

Supported by the love of her family, combined with the cultivation of her passion for the arts in school and her work experience with Destiny's Child, Beyoncé has built her successful career. Everything she's done can be traced back through all of the steps she took. She constructed the brand with years of effort, and it required that she stay in school, build networks, and cultivate a strong fan base. Those actions have gotten her to where she is today.

Text-Dependent Questions:

1. What was the name of the girl group Beyoncé was a member of before it was called Destiny's Child?
2. What high schools did Beyoncé attend?
3. How many singles from Beyoncé's first album made it onto the *Billboard* charts?

Research Project:

This chapter notes that Beyoncé still continued her studies while a member of Destiny's Child. Find what the current high school dropout rate is in your city or state, and if there are any efforts being made in your area to keep students in school. Then research what Beyoncé—and other celebrities she has worked with—say about the importance of education and how it affects personal development.

Why is it important to stay in school, even while pursuing creative or other endeavors?

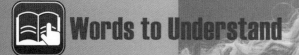

Words to Understand

endorsement: money earned from a product recommendation, typically by a celebrity, athlete, or other public figure.

RIAA Program: The Recording Industry Association of America's Certification Program classifies albums and singles as Gold and Platinum to honor artists, track sales, and stand as benchmarks for success in the industry.

Chapter 3

Beyoncé's Hip-Hop Career, Interests, and Passions in Moments

More Than Just a Musician

Creating and performing music isn't the only avenue that Beyoncé has explored so far. She also has ties to acting and fashion, and has partnered with several organizations for **endorsements**.

The Life of an Actor

Along with her robust career as a singer, Beyoncé has several film projects on her resume. She has acted in and voiced animated characters for a total of ten different films between 2001 and 2013. One notable role was playing Deena Jones in *Dreamgirls*, a film remake of the Broadway play. She was nominated for a Golden Globe for her portrayal.

There have been reports that Beyoncé will be the voice of a character, as well as producing the music, in Disney's upcoming live-action remake of *The Lion King*. Though the reports are yet to be confirmed, her fans are extremely excited at the prospect—highlighting that her work in film continues to be popular.

Fashion Lines

House of Dereon

Along with her mother, Tina Knowles, Beyoncé produced a ready-to-wear fashion line in 2006. It was discontinued in 2012, after years of providing women and girls with a number of casual and formal clothing options. The line was named for Beyoncé's maternal grandmother, Agnes Dereon.

IVY PARK

In April 2016, Beyoncé launched an athletic wear clothing line in partnership with Topshop's owner, Sir Phillip Green. The joint venture sells over 200 different types of athletic clothing all over the world. Items are available online and at several retailers around the world, including Topshop, Nordstrom, Hudson's Bay, and Revolve. Clothing items sell anywhere between $30 and $200.

Tina Knowles

Beyoncé Heat

Along with her clothing collections, Beyoncé has also launched her own fragrance line called Beyoncé Heat. She sells nine different scents in total—Heat, Heat Rush, Midnight Heat, Shimmering Heat, Rise, and Pulse are the names of some of these perfumes. The fragrances are available to purchase online and at retailers like Kohl's, Sears, and Walgreens.

Her first perfume release managed to break Macy's sales record by ringing up $75,000 worth of sales in one day. Reports indicate that Beyoncé has made over $400 million through her perfumes.

Endorsements

Fragrances

Alongside her own fragrances, Beyoncé partnered with Tommy Hilfiger to launch the perfume True Star in 2004. She was paid $250,000 for the partnership, and to represent and promote the fragrance. The advertisements involved her singing *Wishing on a Star* a capella, along with print advertisements.

Beyoncé excitedly expressed her thoughts about the experience with the partnership. *"I'm so thrilled, it's so exciting to be a part of this. There's not many women in the world who can say they have their own fragrance, not many black women, so this is wonderful. It's so classy and so timeless and so beautiful."*

Beyoncé also starred in an advertisement for Emporio Armani's perfume Diamonds. The endorsement campaign featured Beyoncé singing *Diamonds Are a Girl's Best Friend*.

Fast Fact 2:

Artists with the Most Number One Singles in *Billboard* History: **Rihanna**—

After her single *Work* reached number one on the *Billboard* charts, Rihanna became the artist with the third most number one hits of all time, with fourteen number one hits. Before that, Rihanna was tied with Michael Jackson, who had thirteen number one singles. She is only behind Mariah Carey currently (who has eighteen number one hits), and The Beatles (who had twenty top singles).

Pepsi

Beyoncé partnered with Pepsi in a $50 million deal in 2012. She appeared in a number of Pepsi ads since 2002, prior to this deal. Part of this campaign included performing in the Super Bowl in 2013, being featured on exclusive, limited-edition Pepsi cans, and musical endeavors. In 2013, she was featured in a Pepsi commercial singing her song, *Grown Woman*. Though it wasn't an official single from her album, it was an exciting sneak peek and preview for her new music.

Super Bowl 2012's stage performance of Music by Madonna

About the *Grown* Woman advertising project, she said, *"I had so much fun collaborating on this campaign with Pepsi. I got to re-live some of my favorite past characters and looks."*

Tidal

Beyoncé is a co-owner in the music-streaming company Tidal, which is run by her husband, Jay-Z. The service has approximately 1 million paying users and boasts of having exclusive content from Beyoncé, as well as other hip-hop stars like Nicki Minaj and Kanye West.

Scan to watch *Formation,* which won the Grammy for Best Music Video in 2016 and multiple MTV Music Awards in 2016

Awards Won

Both as a solo artist and as a member of Destiny's Child, Beyoncé has won over 280 awards to date, and has been nominated for over 800 awards worldwide. As of the 59th Grammy Awards, she's been nominated for sixty-three Grammy Awards, which are more nominations than any other female artist. To add to that already-impressive number, she has won twenty-two Grammys—the second largest number of wins for a female artist.

Her vast number of awards and nominations come from songs, tours, albums, acting, musical collaborations, and the fashion industry. Here is a partial list of some of her most impressive and well-deserved wins:

Grammy Awards

Best Urban Contemporary Album—LEMONDADE | Won in 2016

Best Music Video—*Formation* | Won in 2016

Best R&B Performance, Best R&B Song—*Drunk in Love* | Won in 2014

Best Surround Sound Album—BEYONCÉ | Won in 2014

Best Traditional R&B Performance—*Love on Top* | Won in 2012

Song of the Year—*Single Ladies (Put a Ring on It)* | Won in 2009

Best Female Pop Vocal Performance—*Halo* | Won in 2009

Best Female R&B Vocal Performance—*Single Ladies (Put a Ring on It)* | Won in 2009

Best Traditional R&B Vocal Performance—*At Last* | Won in 2009

Best R&B Song—*Single Ladies (Put a Ring on It)* | Won in 2009

Best Contemporary R&B Album—I AM... SASHA FIERCE | Won in 2009

Best Contemporary R&B Album—B'DAY | Won in 2006

American Music Awards

Tour of the Year—The *Formation* World Tour | Won in 2016

Favorite Soul/R&B Album—BEYONCÉ | Won in 2014

Favorite Soul/R&B Female Artist | Won in 2009, 2011, 2012, and 2014

International Artist Award | Won in 2007

BET Awards

Album of the Year—LEMONDADE | Won in 2017

Video Director of the Year—*Sorry*, featuring Kahil Joseph | Won in 2017

Video of the Year—*Formation* | Won in 2016

Video of the Year—*7/11* | Won in 2015

Best Collaboration—*Drunk in Love*, featuring Jay-Z | Won in 2014

Video of the Year—*Telephone*, featuring Lady Gaga | Won in 2010

Video of the Year—*Single Ladies (Put a Ring on It)* | Won in 2009

Best Female R&B Artist | Won in 2009, 2012, 2014, 2015, 2016, and 2017

Video of the Year—*Irreplaceable* | Won in 2007

Best Female R&B Artist | Won in 2007

Best Collaboration—*Crazy in Love*, featuring Jay-Z | Won in 2004

Best Female R&B Artist | Won in 2004

Beyoncé

Billboard Awards

Top R&B Album—LEMONDADE | Won in 2017

Top R&B Artist | Won in 2017

Top Touring Artist | Won in 2017

Top Female Artist | Won in 2017

Top R&B Album—4 | Won in 2012

Billboard Woman of the Year Award | Won in 2009

New R&B Artist | Won in 2003

New Female Artist | Won in 2003

BRIT Awards

Best International Female Solo Artist | Won in 2004 and 2017

Glamour Magazine Woman of the Year

International Solo Artist of the Year | Won in 2007

Guinness Book of World Records

Most-Liked Instagram Picture | Won in 2017

Fastest-Selling Album on iTunes—BEYONCÉ | Won in 2013

Highest Annual Earnings by a Female Singer | Won in 2008

MTV Awards

Breakthrough Long Form—LEMONADE | Won in 2016

Best Female Video—*Hold Up* | Won in 2016

Video of the Year, Best Pop Video, Best Direction, Best Cinematography in a Video, Best Editing in a Video, Best Choreography in a Video—*Formation* | Won in 2016

Best Cinematography in a Video, Best Video with a Social Message—
Pretty Hurts | Won in 2014

Best Editing in a Video—*Countdown* | Won in 2012

Best Choreography in a Video—*Run the World (Girls)* | Won in 2011

Video of the Year, Best Choreography in a Video—
Single Ladies (Put a Ring on It) | Won in 2009

Most Earthshattering Collaboration—*Beautiful Liar,* featuring Shakira | Won in 2007

Best R&B Video—*Check on It*, featuring Slim Thug | Won in 2006

Best Female Video—*Naughty Girl* | Won in 2004

Best Female Video, Best R&B Video, Best Choreography in a Video—
Crazy in Love, featuring Jay-Z | Won in 2003

NAACP Image Awards

Entertainer of the Year | Won in 2004

Outstanding Female Artist | Won in 2009, 2014, and 2017

People's Choice Awards

Favorite Female Performer | Won in 2004

Peabody Awards

Entertainment—LEMONDADE | Won in 2017

Council of Fashion Designers of America

Fashion Icon | Won in 2016

Beyoncé

Success Doesn't Happen Overnight

Versatile, hardworking, determined, and successful are just a few words that can be used to describe Beyoncé and the tremendous amount of work she's done. From designing and producing visual masterpieces through her music to establishing her own fashion lines, Beyoncé has worked hard to create success. She finds fascinating new ventures and gives it her all. It's always exciting to see what she might do next. This versatility comes from how hard she's worked in the industry—since she was a child—and how she continues to find projects that she's passionate about.

One thing we can all learn from Beyoncé's hard work is to never give up on our dreams—because hard work does pay off.

Text-Dependent Questions:

1. Of the various projects listed in the chapter, name two that Beyoncé has participated in outside of music.

2. Which of Beyoncé's albums were also visual albums?

3. Name three artists that Beyoncé has collaborated with more than once.

Research Project:

Research the music certification industry in the United States (**the RIAA**) and two other countries in the world. What is the highest honor that an artist can receive in the United States and in the other countries you selected? What does it take for a single to become number one in each of these countries? Comment on any similarities or differences you notice between the certifying companies. Note the number of times Beyoncé has received the highest honors in countries you selected. What does your research say about her global impact as a celebrity?

Words to Understand

brand: a particular product or a characteristic that serves to identify a particular product; a brand name is one having a well-known and usually highly regarded or marketable word or phrase.

marketing: the process or technique of promoting, selling, and distributing a product or service.

press conference: an interview or announcement given by a public figure to the press at an appointed time.

representation: how words used by the media present gender, age, ethnicity, national and regional identity, social issues, and events to an audience; these media texts have the power to shape an audience's knowledge, understanding, and feelings about important topics.

word of mouth: informal oral communication—a marketing tactic that involves consumers voluntarily sharing information about a product with other consumers.

Chapter 4

Beyoncé's Brand Messaging— Becoming a Household Name

Beyoncé's Marketing Strategy

Words matter, and the meaning behind the stories we tell has an impact beyond just one moment. That's one aspect of storytelling that marketers are extremely familiar with. Understanding the approaches that Beyoncé takes when it comes to **marketing** her content, her **brand**, and her work tells us about the kind of person she is and the public brand image she hopes to portray. Three key approaches to her marketing strategy are using social media, promoting her work through buzz marketing, and using exclusivity.

Social Media Tactics

Beyoncé has 15 million followers on Twitter, more than 64 million followers on Facebook, and 106 million followers on Instagram. In July 2017, Beyoncé broke Instagram records by posting a photo of her newborn twins. This photo became the Most-Liked photo in Instagram history, with over 10 million likes. The number of likes proves that Beyoncé has a strong following and a clear fan base dedicated to everything she posts.

Leveraging her high number of social media followers is an important part of Beyoncé's marketing strategy. Every new offering results in millions of views, comments, and likes. Along with fan comments, several media outlets often promote her posts by discussing and featuring her photos and announcements in their articles and shows, which further increases the number of views her posts receive. Additionally, fans and other celebrities imitate her photos not only because they receive so much attention but also to celebrate their appreciation of her. This became extremely clear after the posts she made focusing on her pregnancy with Sir Carter and Rumi.

Through Instagram, Beyoncé connects with her followers by giving them glimpses into her personal life. Photos of her family, events she attends, her outfits, and photos chronicling her pregnancy all gave fans a close, personal look at her life. She typically controls the Instagram account herself, so the information comes directly from her and highlights events occurring in her life as they happen.

Her marketing team uses Facebook for more promotional messages about Beyoncé's music, charity initiatives, and upcoming events. They're careful to make sure the messages sound natural and meaningful. Twitter isn't a large part of Beyoncé's social media strategy—currently, the account has a total of ten tweets, as only major announcements are posted through Twitter.

One notable aspect of her plans for using social media is embodied in the statement "less is more." When updates happen too frequently, they can be overwhelming to followers, or lose their meaning. However, when they're less frequent, fans more deeply appreciate the moments that are posted. Similarly, Beyoncé doesn't often caption her Instagram photos—she lets the photo speak for itself. When she does decide to caption one, her comment stands out more among fans and the media. This minimalistic approach lets Beyoncé control the personal messages that she shares with her fans through social media, and keeps them interested.

Beyoncé has been known for keeping her personal life private, so she uses social media strategically and is able to connect with fans in a new way through her accounts. The story she shares through these reminds fans that she's a real, honest person who has a flair for elegance and loves her family.

No Promotion Strategies

Beyoncé has been in the public eye since 1990. For years, she has cultivated her image and brand as a strong, hardworking, and talented woman. All of this hard work has paid off in a rare and useful process—she no longer needs to promote her work in the traditional way. Typically, prior to an album launch, artists must spend weeks, or even months, on a press tour. They conduct interviews on talk shows, perform and release various singles on those shows, and conduct **press conferences** or press releases to promote the upcoming albums. Then, following the actual launch, they have to continue to promote new singles and music videos from the album.

Buzz Marketing

Beyoncé has become a public figure with such a strong following and fan base that she doesn't need to follow this traditional approach. In fact, the lack of marketing and promotion prior to album release actually adds to the buzz and hype surrounding them immediately afterward. This buzz contributes to sales and promotions without Beyoncé or her team having to do any direct promotion work.

"Buzz" can also be described as "**word of mouth**"—an element that involves people talking about her work and recommending the music to each other, instead of the music being directly promoted or marketed to them in a traditional way.

Surprise

In 2013, Beyoncé unveiled her self-titled visual album with no promotion, releasing it as a surprise project. That action has been lauded as one of the most brilliant ideas in music history. It created a natural buzz because of the shock, surprise, and excitement that fans experienced in the process of first hearing about the album's sudden availability.

It sold 80,000 copies in three hours, and there were reports of the iTunes website crashing because of the number of people attempting to access it. The only real promotion Beyoncé engaged in was posting about the album on her Instagram account—a video with snapshots of the album and the caption "Surprise!" The announcement gained over 620,000 likes.

Of course, behind the scenes of this release, there was tremendous planning. This preparation would have included the timing of posts and what to include in them, along with the work it took to keep recording and filming sessions a secret. The end result, however, was a seamless, completely unexpected album release, one that still gets talked about to this day as an incredible example of **marketing**, and as evidence of Beyoncé's star power.

Other artists have attempted to employ similar surprise strategies, but because Beyoncé has been so successful in making it her own, they are often called "copycats" and they are rarely as successful. Sales executives argue that if other artists attempt to use this kind of strategy, some of the buzz wears off because it's not a new tactic anymore.

Several things worked to Beyoncé's advantage in releasing her self-titled album as a surprise, including an already-strong fan base, years of support, a number of successful albums and tours in the past, and a strong sense of anticipation among fans for her

next piece of work. Other artists find it hard to have all the same parts in order the same way, which means the strategy is almost impossible to mimic. It is very strongly linked to her brand name. Any other artist who tries to use such a strategy will always be compared to Beyoncé—forever linking her brand to the concept of "no promotion" marketing.

Using Exclusivity as an Advantage

Alongside a minimalistic approach in her social media and marketing efforts, exclusivity is another aspect that adds value to her work. The scarcity principle is often used in marketing in an effort to demonstrate that a product is of high quality and to encourage

consumers to make a purchase quickly. Buyers are more inclined to want to purchase a product if the item is rare, or if it will only be available for a short period of time. Since the freedom to purchase an item is threatened, people want to possess the item immediately, or as soon as possible.

By adopting aspects of the scarcity principle, Beyoncé has used the idea of exclusivity to sell her latest album, LEMONADE. After the film aired on HBO, the footage and songs were released exclusively to be streamed on Tidal. For a period of time, Tidal was the only location where people could stream and view the album in its entirety.

Beyoncé has since released some of the tracks and videos on YouTube, and the songs are available for purchase on iTunes, though Tidal is still the only place where people are able to see the entire film. Also, the album is currently not available on Spotify—another popular streaming site. The exclusive access on Tidal, immediately following LEMONADE's release, was a move that directed people to the streaming service that Beyoncé has ties to, making it a smart business decision. Knowing there was only one place to stream the visual album motivated people to create a Tidal account to see Beyoncé's latest work.

Scan here to watch Beyoncé's acceptance speech for Best Urban Contemporary Album at the 2016 Grammy Awards

Beyoncé is also selling a LEMONADE boxed set through her website, in limited quantities. The set comes with a collector's edition coffee table book, a double vinyl LP, and audio and visual album downloads. The hardcover book includes never-before-seen photos from the making of Lemonade, depicts the themes and inspiration for various moments in the film, and includes Beyoncé's personal writing and lyrics. This is a deeply personal collector's boxed set that includes unique and exclusive information not shared anywhere else. This exclusivity generates fan motivation to purchase the $299.99 boxed set. The marketing campaign employs the concepts of scarcity and exclusivity by highlighting there will only be a limited number of copies available, and by showcasing the fact there is information in the set that is not available anywhere else, like the behind-the-scenes photos.

Award Speeches—Messages Matter

Beyoncé at the Grammys: Why Representation Is Valuable

When it comes to winning awards and giving speeches, Beyoncé knows how to tell a story and connect with her audience on a personal and fundamental level. When she won the Grammy for Best Urban Contemporary Album at the 2016 Grammy Awards, her speech pointed out the importance of **representation** in media. She also discussed personally finding growth and confronting issues of pain and discomfort.

In her speech, one notable moment was when she explained her motivations for creating LEMONADE:

"We all experience pain and loss, and often we become inaudible. My intention for the film and album was to create a body of work that would give a voice to our pain, our struggles, our darkness and our history. To confront issues that make us uncomfortable. It's important to me to show images to my children that reflect their beauty, so they can grow up in a world where they look in the mirror, first through their own families—as well as the news, the Super Bowl, the Olympics, the White House, and the Grammys—and see themselves, and have no doubt that they're beautiful, intelligent, and capable. This is something I want for every child of every race. And I feel it's vital that we learn from the past and recognize our tendencies to repeat our mistakes."

Scan the code here to view Beyoncé's acceptance speech at the 2016 Council of Fashion Designers of America

Telling a Story through a Speech: Winning "Fashion Icon Award"

One of Beyoncé's most personal and poignant speeches happened when she won the Fashion Icon Award from the Council of Fashion Designers of America. She told a very profound story of her grandmother being a seamstress in a tearful, heartfelt acceptance speech. She shared how her grandmother

Fast Fact 4:

Women Lifting Each Other Up—At

the 2016 Grammy Awards, Adele won the award for Album of the Year. During her acceptance speech, she dedicated the award to Beyoncé, even going so far as to break the award in half, claiming that Beyoncé was the "artist of her life."

Scan here to watch Adele's entire acceptance speech

sewed to pay for her mother's schooling fees, and how her mother sewed her clothes, and outfits for Destiny's Child. Other designers weren't interested in creating for them, and they couldn't afford expensive outfits. She recalled that wearing the costumes designed by her mother felt like "an extra suit of armor."

The award acceptance speech provided an opportunity for Beyoncé to share a deeply personal reality, and also highlighted how far-reaching her impact is. She doesn't make a difference just in the music industry, but also has noteworthy successes and moments in other industries as well, like the fashion industry.

Brand Messaging and Public Relations with Beyoncé

Beyoncé's star power means that she has cultivated a strong relationship with her fans through social media, promotion initiatives, and award speeches. She shares snapshots of her personal life story through each of these mediums, revealing a little bit more as time passes. Fans appreciate each new fact they learn about her, and wait patiently for the next piece of the puzzle to emerge. Due to this strong bond between Beyoncé, her fans, and the media, it's clear that her actions will continue to surprise and excite people for years to come. Each new initiative she designs will communicate a new bit of information about her to fans, which will work to continue building her brand and her public persona.

Text-Dependent Questions:

❶ How many followers does Beyoncé have on Instagram?

❷ What award did Adele dedicate to Beyoncé at the 2016 Grammys?

❸ Why does Beyoncé's "no promotion" strategy work?

Research Project:

Research some of Beyoncé's interviews, press conferences, or award acceptance speeches, and find one speech that truly resonates with you. What in particular did she say that connected to you? Comment on her style of speech—what type of tone or style did she use? Was she conversational or more professional? Was her tone and style effective in conveying the meaning behind her speech? Finally, discuss whether there are elements of her style that you may consider using in any of your own public speaking endeavors.

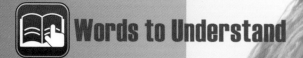

Words to Understand

feminism: the theory of the political, economic, and social equality of the sexes.

philanthropy: goodwill to fellow members of the human race; an active effort to promote human welfare.

racism: a belief or doctrine that inherent differences among the various human racial groups determine cultural or individual achievement, usually involving the idea that one's own race is superior and has the right to dominate others, or that a particular racial group is inferior to others.

sexism: discrimination or devaluation based on a person's sex or gender, as in restricted job opportunities, especially such discrimination directed against women.

social responsibility: an ethical framework that suggests that an entity, whether it be an organization or individual, has an obligation to act for the benefit of society at large.

Chapter 5:

Beyoncé Reminds Us to Be Good

Charitable Work: Giving Back to the Community

Beyoncé has been targeted countless of times with inaccurate claims that she hasn't participated in charitable initiatives throughout her career. In 2012, she received a blow from a celebrity and fellow singer, Harry Belafonte. He argued that she had "turn[ed] [her] back on **social responsibility.**" However, this was an error, as evidenced by her representatives. They responded with a list of the "unselfish work" that Beyoncé has completed—ranging from performing in benefit concerts to founding charity initiatives, and donating $100,000 to victims of Hurricane Ike.

Beyoncé always finds time to give back to her community. In fact, her giving spirit and work as a champion for social change resulted in her being named DoSomething.Org's Most Charitable Celebrity in 2016. Her work in co-founding The Survivor Foundation and founding the BeyGOOD Foundation are particularly noteworthy.

The Survivor Foundation

One of Beyoncé's earliest charity initiatives was The Survivor Foundation. Founded in 2005 with singer Kelly Rowland, her parents Matthew and Tina Knowles, and her sister Solange, the foundation aimed to help individuals affected by Hurricane Katrina. It focused on providing temporary housing to the victims displaced by the natural disaster. In addition, Beyoncé supported The Survivor Foundation by holding food drives during her 2006 music tour. Beyoncé didn't just create the foundation—she integrated it into her musical career, fully demonstrating her dedication to giving back.

BeyGOOD Foundation

Beyoncé's international charitable foundation, BeyGOOD, was founded in 2013, and has since launched partnerships with a number of global charities, created scholarships, hosted charity music events, and more. In 2014, it reached more than 2 million people through

Fast Fact 5:

Good Deeds with Goodwill—

In 2013, Beyoncé partnered with Goodwill in an effort to tackle unemployment. She wanted to team up with an organization that "puts people first and works every day to help them improve and re-establish their lives."

its partnerships, charity drives, and events. This number and the foundation's global impact continue to grow, and will undoubtedly expand in the future.

Formation Scholars—A Merit Scholarship Program for Academic Year 2017–2018

In April 2017, to celebrate the one-year anniversary of her critically acclaimed album LEMONADE being released, Beyoncé announced a new initiative through BeyGOOD called Formation Scholars. This merit-based scholarship awarded four women with $25,000 to pursue education in creative arts, music, literature, and African-American studies. It provided these confident, bold young women with the opportunity to further pursue their educational and professional goals. Winners were selected based on an essay submission describing how LEMONADE affected their academic achievement and their education.

BEYGOOD4BURUNDI—Solving the Water Crisis in Burundi

BeyGOOD launched the campaign "BeyGOOD4Burundi" in June 2017. The project is working in partnership with UNICEF, a United Nations organization concerned with improving the health and nutrition of children and mothers throughout the world. The initiative itself focuses on bringing clean water to Burundi, one of the most populated regions in Africa.

Burundi

Individuals can donate directly to the campaign, or purchase special edition merchandise, like t-shirts sold on Beyoncé's website. One hundred percent of the profits from the sale of these items go toward supporting this project.

In Burundi, approximately half the population lacks access to clean and safe drinking water. The partnership will use the funds donated to "support building water supply systems for healthcare facilities and schools, and the drilling of boreholes, wells and springs to bring safe water to districts." The work will provide about half a million people in Burundi with access to safe water.

Fast Fact 6:

Access to Clean Water— Research in 2015 showed that 663 million people, or one in ten people, drank water from unprotected sources. Almost half of these individuals lived in sub-Saharan Africa.

Music for Giving—How Beyoncé Uses Music to Give Back

Beyoncé doesn't just use her partnerships through charitable foundations to support the community. As she did with The Survivor Foundation, Beyoncé finds new and interesting ways to align her musical career with her **philanthropic** work. From participating in charity concerts to fully aligning her *Formation* World Tour with three global nonprofit organizations, Beyoncé works hard—not only to sell popular music, but to promote community engagement and instill the value of giving back to her fans.

Concerts for Charity

Beyoncé headlined the Tidal X: 1015, a charity show that occurred in October 2016 at the Barclays Center. The event was also streamed live on Tidal, the website best known for being created by her husband, Jay-Z. The charity concert was held in support of the Robin Hood Foundation, an organization committed to providing education for children in New York City, along with other charity groups nominated by the artists who were to perform. This concert was a continuation of the previous year's Tidal X: 1020. Proceeds from the 2015 concert were distributed to grassroots and nonprofit organizations committed to fighting social injustices.

Formation World Tour

During this world tour, Beyoncé not only shared her musical talents but also motivated fans to give back through a number of initiatives. First, she encouraged her fans to donate to through her website as they purchased tickets to her *Formation* World Tour. Through this, she helped to raise over $82,000 to support the water crisis in Flint, Michigan.

Additionally, throughout her *Formation* World Tour, she partnered with three global charities through her charity foundation, BeyGOOD. The charities selected included the United Way Worldwide, Chime for Change, and Global Citizen. Each was required to have a presence during her tour stops. Fans were able to learn more about the organizations and donate—both onsite at the tour and online. At each tour stop, fans who donated to United Way Worldwide were also entered into a VIP ticket contest. Proceeds from this ticket contest were donated to organizations fighting the Flint water crisis by United Way Worldwide. Clearly, Beyoncé looked for several new and exciting ways to get her fans enthusiastic about giving back—and did so all within the bounds of her musical expertise and her world tour.

Finally, fans were invited to attend an additional event at three stops on the tour—Houston, Compton, and Detroit. In Houston, the occasion focused on combating hunger in the city. The Compton tour stop event benefited the Urban Education Institute, an organization committed to improving education for K–12 urban students, while the special program held in Detroit focused on water crisis efforts in Flint, Michigan.

By putting in the extra effort to create special events that highlighted lesser-known initiatives, Beyoncé was able to fully connect herself with organizations committed to the greater good of the world. She increased the charities' exposure and showed fans how they could give back within their own communities, all while enjoying her music.

Rising above and against Hatred

Beyond her charitable work, if there's one thing we can learn from Beyoncé, it's to rise above hatred. It's unfortunate and unfair that she must deal with the **racism** and **sexism** prevalent in the music industry. On Twitter, twice she has mentioned these issues and the systemic barriers she must cross. The responses to those posts are riddled with

extreme voices of hate from people who refuse to acknowledge the hard work she puts in, and people mocking her appearance through racist and sexist harassment.

Beyoncé finds ways to love and support her community, even if part of this community doesn't respond. She rises above the vitriol and navigates through these difficult situations bravely, inspiring the next generation of musicians and young creatives to do the same. In her own words, she says, *"When I'm not feeling my best I ask myself, 'What are you gonna do about it?' I use the negativity to fuel the transformation into a better me."*

Inspiration through Music

Beyoncé's hit song and video, *Pretty Hurts*, was a feminist message expressing a commentary on how society views beauty. In a behind-the-scenes film about this music video, Beyoncé's words are inspiring and sharp. She specifically chose Melina Matsoukas to direct the video, as she felt that this director in particular would understand the vision she had in mind. Melina points out that the song (and music video) aims to expose the extremes that women go through in order to appear physically beautiful.

Scan here to watch the behind-the-scenes video of the *Pretty Hurts* taping

In the behind-the-scenes film, Melina goes on to mention that outer beauty doesn't bring happiness, but rather, finding one's true self is what brings that joy. Beyoncé's choice to depict this message and work with a director who could bring this message to life in the *Pretty Hurts* video is just one example of how Beyoncé uses her music to deliver needed social commentary. This reflection, delivered to fans in the form of a heartfelt video, has the effect of inspiring them to search for their beauty within instead of focusing on unhealthy ideals of outer beauty.

It is also one way that Beyoncé brings her own personal experiences into her music in a manner that connects with her fans and brings them into an understanding of important life lessons. Through her difficulties, and her bravery in representing difficult, emotional stories, others are able to grow and learn.

Another song of Beyoncé's that has received strong praise for highlighting positive and empowering themes is ***Flawless*. The first portion of the song features a quote from novelist Chimamanda Ngozi Adichie. The quote defines **feminism** and describes ways that girls are systematically treated as "less than boys." In creating a song that empowers girls and reminds them that they are "flawless," Beyoncé brings a new message to girls who are ignored or mistreated. She tells them that they are valued, just as they are.

It's important to note that the song, though it does specifically deal with feminism, is one that can be enjoyed by everyone. That's part of the beauty of Beyoncé's music—it's catchy, upbeat, and intelligent, so that everybody is able to glean something from it.

LEMONADE, Beyoncé's visual album, has been lauded for depicting her deeply personal journey. It's emotional, and highlights her growth in interpersonal relationships. From dealing with being in the public eye to experiencing adultery, through LEMONADE, Beyoncé has bared a part of her soul with fans. It was critically acclaimed for a reason, as it connected to viewers on a very intimate level. In showing her fans some of the difficulties she has faced in the past through her music, she encourages them to learn from her journey and grow along with her. By learning about her personal development, fans are able to embark on their own individual journeys, sparked by her inspiring and original music.

Formation, Beyoncé's critically acclaimed single off her LEMONADE album, featured a number of social justice themes. She combated police brutality by featuring "Mothers of the Movement"—mothers who have lost their children in high-profile shootings—holding photos of their late sons. The song has also been lauded as a feminist anthem, especially for African-American women, who are often left out of media representation in television and movies. Creating music that empowers people who are hurt, and feel alone, is another way that Beyoncé inspires and motivates entire generations of people to rise above difficult experiences.

How Beyoncé Reminds Us to BeyGOOD

With her BeyGOOD Foundation charitable work and her inspiring music, Beyoncé teaches her fans and the general public to work hard and work positively. Even through personal and professional struggles,

Beyoncé finds a way to rise above the difficulties and finds time to give back to her community. Her work serves as a reminder to us all to be kind, helpful, and, above all, to be good.

Text-Dependent Questions:

1. What are some of the ways listed in the chapter that the BeyGOOD Foundation participates in philanthropic initiatives?
2. There were three foundations that Beyoncé aligned with during her *Formation* World Tour. Which one was also part of an additional VIP ticket contest?
3. In what ways does Beyoncé's music give back to her fans and the community at large?

Research Project:

Beyoncé's career has spanned several years, starting as a member of Destiny's Child. Since then, she has released six musical albums, participated in five headlining tours, and starred in a number of films. She's a mother, a wife, and successful hip-hop star. With all of that on her resume, she has also participated in numerous charity initiatives, always remembering to give back. For this project, select two or three of her philanthropic projects—in music, film, or with charitable organizations—that you believe have benefited the community in the most positive way. Explain each project's intent and impact, and why you think it had a positive effect on the community at large. Think about ways that you could implement some of Beyoncé's initiatives in your own neighborhood. Select one of the projects you highlighted and explain possible ways you could further its effect nearby.

Series Glossary of Key Terms

A&R: an abbreviation that stands for Artists and Repertoire, which is a record company department responsible for the recruitment and development of talent; similar to a talent scout for sports.

ambient: a musical style that relies on electronic sounds, gentle music, and the lack of a regular beat to create a relaxed mood for the listener.

brand: a particular product or a characteristic that serves to identify a particular product; a brand name is one having a well-known and usually highly regarded or marketable word or phrase.

cameo: also called a cameo role; a minor part played by a prominent performer in a single scene of a motion picture or a television show.

choreography: the art of planning and arranging the movements, steps, and patterns of dancers.

collaboration: a product created by working with someone else; combining individual talents.

debut: a first public appearance on a stage, on television, or so on, or the beginning of a profession or career; the first appearance of something, like a new product.

deejay (DJ): a slang term for a person who spins vinyl records on a turntable; aka a disc jockey.

demo: a recording of a new song, or of one performed by an unknown singer or group, distributed to disc jockeys, recording companies, and the like, to demonstrate the merits of the song or performer.

dubbed: something that is named or given a new name or title; in movies, when the actors' voices have been replaced with those of different performers speaking another language; in music, transfer or copying of previously recorded audio material from one medium to another.

endorsement: money earned from a product recommendation, typically by a celebrity, athlete, or other public figure.

entrepreneur: a person who organizes and manages any enterprise, especially a business, usually with considerable initiative and at financial risk.

falsetto: a man singing in an unnaturally high voice, accomplished by creating a vibration at the very edge of the vocal chords.

genre: a subgroup or category within a classification, typically associated with works of art, such as music or literature.

hone, honing: sharpening or refining a set of skills necessary to achieve success or perform a specific task.

icon: a symbol that represents something, such as a team, a religious person, a location, or an idea.

innovation: the introduction of something new or different; a brand-new feature or upgrade to an existing idea, method, or item.

instrumental: serving as a crucial means, agent, or tool; of, relating to, or done with an instrument or tool.

jingle: a short verse, tune, or slogan used in advertising to make a product easily remembered.

mogul: someone considered to be very important, powerful, and in charge; a term usually associated with heads of businesses in the television, movie studio, or recording industries.

performing arts: skills that require public performance, as acting, singing, or dancing.

philanthropy: goodwill to fellow members of the human race; an active effort to promote human welfare.

public relations: the activity or job of providing information about a particular person or organization to the public so that people will regard that person or organization in a favorable way.

sampler: a digital or electronic musical instrument, related to a synthesizer, that uses samples, or sound recordings, of real instruments (trumpet, violin, piano, etc.) mixed with excerpts of recorded songs and other interesting sounds (sirens, ocean waves, construction noises, car horns, etc.) that are stored digitally and can be replayed by a triggering device, like a sequencer, electronic drums, or a MIDI keyboard.

single: a music recording having two or more tracks that is shorter than an album, EP, or LP; also, a song that is particularly popular, independent of other songs on the same album or by the same artist.

Further Reading

Knowles, Beyoncé, Kelly Rowland, and Michelle Williams. *Soul Survivors: The Official Autobiography of Destiny's Child.* Harper Collins Publisher, 2002.

Pointer, Anna. *Beyoncé: Running the World: The Biography,* Coronet. 2015.

Roberts, Chris. *Beyoncégraphica: A Graphic Biography of Beyoncé,* Aurum Press. 2017.

Schnall, Marianne. *What Will It Take to Make a Woman President? Conversations about Women, Leadership, and Power,* Seal Press. 2013.

Taraborrelli, J. Randy. *Becoming Beyoncé: The Untold Story.* Grand Central Publishing, 2015.

Trier-Bieniek, Adrienne. *The Beyoncé Effect: Essays on Sexuality, Race, and Feminism.* McFarland, 2016.

Internet Sources

www.billboard.com
The official site of *Billboard Music*, with articles about artists, chart information, and more.

www.thefader.com/
Official website for a popular New York City–based music magazine.

www.hiphopweekly.com
A young adult hip-hop magazine.

www.thesource.com/
Website for a bi-monthly magazine that covers hip-hop and pop culture.

www.vibe.com/
Music and entertainment website and a member of *Billboard Music*, a division of Billboard-Hollywood Reporter Media Group.

www.beyonce.com/
Beyoncé's official website—the go-to source for all official news, updates, and information.

Citations

Alvarez, Gabriel. "Beyoncé: Mighty Fly (2011 Cover Story & Gallery)." *Complex*. October 20, 2016.

Augustin, Camille. "Alicia Keys Shares What Happened to the 'Put It in a Love Song' Video." *Vibe*. May 13, 2016.

Boone, John. "Beyoncé Says 'Proudest Moment' Was Giving Birth to Blue Ivy, Reveals Who Her Biggest Hero Is." ET Online. March 10, 2016.

Jessen, Monique, and Stephen M. Silverman. "Beyoncé Launches New True Star Fragrance." PEOPLE.com. June 22, 2004.

Ramirez, Erika. "Beyoncé Previews New Song, 'Grown Woman,' in Pepsi Commercial." *Billboard*. April 04, 2013.

Watercutter, Angela. "Beyoncé's Surprise Album Was the Year's Most Brilliant Release." Wired.com. December 13, 2013.

Russonello, Giovanni. "Beyoncé's and Adele's Grammy Speeches: Transcripts." *New York Times*. February 12, 2017.

Romeyn, Kathryn. "CFDA Awards: Beyoncé Recalls How Her Mom's Designs Felt Like an 'Extra Suit of Armor'." *Billboard*. June 07, 2016.

Citations

Little, Lyneka. "Beyoncé's Camp Responds to Belafonte's Criticism She Doesn't Do Enough." *Wall Street Journal*. August 13, 2012.

"BeyGOOD 4 Burundi." *UNICEF USA*. Accessed August 14, 2017. https://www.unicefusa.org/donate/beygood-4-burundi/32391

Rice, Francesca. "Inspiring Beyoncé Quotes." *Marie Claire*. September 07, 2015.

Educational Videos

Chapter 1:

http://x-qr.net/1Gjc
http://x-qr.net/1HLU
http://x-qr.net/1DyG
http://x-qr.net/1HKu
http://x-qr.net/1ECv
http://x-qr.net/1HD8
http://x-qr.net/1DnJ

Chapter 2:

http://x-qr.net/1F2c

Chapter 3:

http://x-qr.net/1HcY

Chapter 4:

http://x-qr.net/1FE0
http://x-qr.net/1DEq
http://x-qr.net/1FJQ

Chapter 5:

http://x-qr.net/1HSK

Index

Index

Index

Photo Credits

Chapter 1:
ID 30012692 © Sbukley | Dreamstime
ID 13795646 © Frescomovie | Dreamstime
ID 36724653 © Carrienelson1 | Dreamstime.com
ID 73843807 © Chiarabenedettacondorelli |
Dreamstime
VisualAlbum.jpg | Wikimedia Commons
Tina_Knowles_and_Beyoncé_cropped.jpg |
Wikimedia Commons
Déjà_Vu_(Beyoncé_Knowles_single_-_cover_
art).jpg | VEVO
beyonce-bts-600.jpg | Wikimedia Commons

Chapter 2:
ID 56565234 © Paul Oliver | Dreamstime
Beyonce_01_cropped.jpg | Flickr
Star_of_Destiny's_Child.jpg | Wikimedia Commons
BookerT-HSforPerfArts.jpg | Wikimedia Commons
beyonce_feat___jay_z____crazy_in_love_by_
other_covers-d6amjcw.jpg | VEVO

Chapter 3:
ID 27559790 © Roystudio | Dreamstime
ID 34073910 © Little_prince | Dreamstime
ID 35296249 © Ivan Mikhaylov | Dreamstime
ID 11828080 © Yury Shirokov | Dreamstime
ID 18066844 © Christin Farmer | Dreamstime
ID 24199127 © Featureflash | Dreamstime
ID 29215732 © Laurence Agron | Dreamstime
ID 45737678 © Jaguarps | Dreamstime
ID 45737738 © Jaguarps | Dreamstime
ID 78568483 © Baloon111 | Dreamstime
ID 103139281 © Andre DurÃo | Dreamstime
ebfa2d61b4fcf66d9ff6157e1b63194f.jpg
Flawless.jpg | Flickr
Superbowl_2012_stage.jpg | Wikimedia Commons
rehost-2016-9-13-88fe5d47-3f27-4ae9-8d8c-
128e5f17b387.jpg | Flickr

Chapter 4:
ID 32585453 © Sbukley | Dreamstime
ID 103139000 © Andre DurÃo | Dreamstime
Beyonce_Michael_Costello_Gown_Grammys.jpg |
Wikimedia Commons
Beyoncé_-_Beyoncé.jpg | Wikimedia Commons
5765878735_7ddc33396c_z.jpg | Flicke
AcceptanceSpeech.jpg | Wikimedia Commons
Adele-Award.jpg | Wikimedia Commons
Another_Beyonce_photo_-_Barcelona_2007.jpg |
Wikimedia Commons
BeyAccept.jpg | Wikimedia Commons
Beyonce_Berlin.jpg | Wikimedia Commons
Beyoncé_Knowles_GMA_2011_cropped.jpg |
Wikimedia Commons
Destiny's_Child_-_Beyoncé_Knowles,_Kelly_
Rowland,_LeToya_Luckett,_Michelle_Williams.jpg
| Wikimedia Commons
Beyonce_Smile.JPG | Wikimedia Commons
Beyonce-2008_cropped.jpg | Wikimedia Commons

Chapter 5:
ID 24306028 © Carrienelson1 | Dreamstime
ID 32457176 © Sbukley | Dreamstime
ID 26885541 © Sbukley | Dreamstime
ID 30010815 © Sbukley | Dreamstime
Karuzi_Burundi_goats.jpg | Flickr
Flickr_-_smilesea_-_Beyoncé_Newcastle_2009_
(6).jpg | Flickr
Beyonce_Knowles_with_necklaces.jpg | Flickr

Author's Biography

Panchami Boyd is a graduate of Western University, and she loves to read, write, listen to music, and travel. She loves to learn new things, and is almost always buried under a new book. Learn more at https://www.writeraccess.com/writer/21187/.